Lists to Live By
— for —
Every Caring Family

COMPILED BY ALICE GRAY,
STEVE STEPHENS, JOHN VAN DIEST

Multnomah® Publishers *Sisters, Oregon*

LISTS TO LIVE BY FOR EVERY CARING FAMILY
published by Multnomah Publishers, Inc.
© 2001 by Alice Gray, Steve Stephens, and John Van Diest
International Standard Book Number: 1-57673-999-6

Cover and interior design by Uttley DouPonce DesignWorks, Sisters, Oregon
Cover image by Eyewire

Scripture quotations are from *The Holy Bible,* New International Version
© 1973, 1984 by International Bible Society,
used by permission of Zondervan Publishing House.

The lists in this book are not substitutes for obtaining professional advice
from qualified persons and organizations. Consult the appropriate professional
advisor for complete and updated information.

For information:
MULTNOMAH PUBLISHERS, INC., POST OFFICE BOX 1720
SISTERS, OREGON 97759

Library of Congress Cataloging-in-Publication Data

Lists to live by for every caring family / compiled by Alice Gray,
Steve Stephens, John Van Diest.
     p. cm.
Includes bibliographical references.
ISBN 1-57673-999-6 (pbk.)
     1. Parenting. 2. Parenting--Religious aspects--Christiaanity. I. Gray, Alice,
1939-- II. Stephens, Steve. III. Van Diest, John.

HQ755.8.L574 2001
649'.1--dc21

                                                        2001000991

01 02 03 04 05 06 07 08 — 10 9 8 7 6 5 4 3 2 1 0

LISTS TO LIVE BY
— *for* —
EVERY CARING FAMILY

Books in the Lists to Live By series:

Contents

Introduction

"Parenting isn't for cowards," says a popular and well-respected psychologist. He's right. Too often, parents feel stressed and overwhelmed . . . and they miss the incredible joy of their children.

Stop.

Sit back.

Relax.

Packed in this little book are easy-to-grasp ideas to help you become the parent you want to be. Wisdom, practical help, and loving suggestions make this a treasured resource that you will turn to again and again for encouragement.

Parenting isn't for cowards, but with a little help it can be a wonderful adventure.

—ALICE GRAY, DR. STEVE STEPHENS, AND JOHN VAN DIEST

Children Learn What They Live

If children live with criticism, they learn to condemn.

If children live with hostility, they learn to fight.

If children live with ridicule, they learn to be shy.

If children live with shame, they learn to be guilty.

If children live with encouragement, they learn confidence.

If children live with tolerance, they learn to be patient.

If children live with praise, they learn to appreciate.

If children live with acceptance, they learn to love.

If children live with approval, they learn to like themselves.

If children live with honesty, they learn truthfulness.

If children live with security,
they learn to have faith in themselves and others.

If children live with friendliness,
they learn the world is a nice place in which to live.

DOROTHY LAW NOLTE
Author of *Children Learn What They Live*

Golden Moments in a Child's Day

1. THE WAKE-UP

   It is important for a child to have some parent-love in the first
   conscious moment of his or her day.

2. THE SEND-OFF

   Horses, Olympians, and children run a good race when they
   get off to a good start. As often as possible, you should be
   there for breakfast and for your child's departure to school.

3. THE RECEPTION

   If you want to get a real reading on how the "game" went,
   you have to be there when the "player" comes off the field.
   Your presence when your child comes in the door says "I love
   you." Your responsibility at the reception is mostly to hug, to
   listen without judgment, to notice your child is home, and to
   be available.

4. THE DEBRIEFING

This may come right after the reception. Kids need to debrief their day—not to be interrogated but to report, celebrate, evaluate, or explode. Again, your role is to listen. Your undivided attention communicates that you care.

5. THE HAPPY ENDING

If "all's well that ends well," it's good for a parent to be there at the end of the day. It's a time for an "I love you," an "I'm sorry," or a "thank you." It puts a period on the end of the day.

RONALD HUTCHCRAFT
From *Five Needs Your Child Must Have Met at Home*

Meaningful Touch

- Hold hands during mealtime prayers.

- Walk one-on-one with each child. Swing hands and talk. Tell jokes. Sing.

- Bad day? Sigh dramatically and say, "I sure could use a great big hug from someone special."

- Wonderful day? Shout, "Hey, everybody! Come hug me! I had the best day!"

- Make Hug Sandwiches. With your spouse, gently surprise unsuspecting children.

- Declare a 100 Hugs Day among your family. Count them as you go.

- Do four-direction kisses: north (foreheads), south (chins), east/west (cheeks).

- Wrap your arms around your children during church and while waiting together or watching TV.

- Apply the Pat Principle: "When in doubt, pat." God made lots of patting places—heads, cheeks, knees, hands, shoulders, backs.

LORRI CARDWELL-CASEY
From *HomeLife* magazine

Qualities to Pass on to Your Children

Determination. "Stick with it, regardless."

Honesty. "Speak and live the truth—always."

Responsibility. "Be dependable, be trustworthy."

Thoughtfulness. "Think of others before yourself."

Confidentiality. "Don't tell secrets. Seal your lips."

Punctuality. "Be on time."

Self-control. "When under stress, stay calm."

Patience. "Fight irritability. Be willing to wait."

Purity. "Reject anything that lowers your standards."

Compassion. "When another hurts, feel it with him."

Diligence. "Work hard. Tough it out."

CHARLES R. SWINDOLL
From *Growing Strong in the Seasons of Life*

12 Things Kids Worry About

1. Will my parents stay together?

2. What if my parents die or get in an accident?

3. How can I keep my mom or dad from getting angry at me?

4. Will people at school like me?

5. Will I be able to do well at school?

6. What if my friends don't want to be my friends anymore?

7. Will my parents be able to pay all our bills?

8. Will I be safe today?

9. Do I look okay?

10. What if I get embarrassed?

11. What if someone hurts me or my family?

12. What does the future hold for me?

MIKE DEBOER
Middle school counselor

Ten Things to Do When Your Child is Afraid

1. *Be close to them.* Just the presence of someone safe is calming.

2. *Touch them.* Holding hands, hugging, rubbing their backs, or any form of reassuring affection helps.

3. *Speak gently and confidently.* Your voice is a point of familiarity and safety, so watch your tone.

4. *Listen to your children.* Let them tell you about their fears, no matter how irrational. Be attentive and patient. Remember, what they say is very important to them.

5. *Tell them something specific to do.* When overwhelmed, taking action helps your children feel that they have power over situations.

6. *Give them positive focuses.* When they think about things that are good or safe or reassuring, fears don't seem so big.

7. *Pray with them.* Seeking God's protection or comfort is something we all need. Remind them that God is always close and He always cares.

8. *Give your children something familiar.* Familiar objects (such as a blanket, photograph, necklace, ring, or stuffed animal) help children relax.

9. *Reassure them that there is always a way out.* Teach them how to solve problems and figure out what to do. Come up with as many solutions as possible. Reassure them that things that seem very frightening now often don't seem so bad in a year or two.

10. *Remind them that we all have fears.* Tell them what frightened you at that age and how you handled it.

DR. STEVE STEPHENS
Author and seminar speaker

Tips to Custom-Fit Your Parenting

Hang out with your kids.

You'll learn who shares, who exhibits a big imagination, and who must be active in order to be happy.

Observe your child's reaction to stressful situations.

What frustrates him? What makes him laugh? How does he respond to teasing? Is he tenderhearted or tough?

Discover talents.

Try lessons in piano, art, or karate, and see what develops: an athletic ability or a creative spirit?

Observe your child's natural speed and capacity for learning and performing.

Can she handle four things at once or only one thing at a time? Does she finish projects on time or is she consistently late?

What brings out your kid's inquisitive nature?

If bugs and spiders mesmerize your daughter, buy her an ant farm. She could be a budding entomologist!

DOTTIE G. BACHTELL
From *Today's Woman* magazine

Be a Parent Teachers Like to See

1. *Establish a positive relationship.* Try to work together. If you become acquainted with your child's teacher before problems occur, you will have a greater impact when a need arises.

2. *Give help, not advice.* Most teachers need help, not more information. When helping, try to do what the teacher wants, not necessarily what you want.

3. *Show appreciation.* Even in the most positive schools, an amazingly small number of parents (and students!) ever show appreciation. We all work harder for those who say thanks.

4. *Be positive.* If your child struggles, make the teacher aware of the problem and ask for suggestions. Don't be afraid to tell the

teacher your plans and how she can help. Focus on changing your child—not the teacher, the school, or the child in the next seat.

5. *Pick your battles.* Don't overlook important issues, but choose your battles carefully. Realize that if you fight, people get hurt. Is it worth it? Many battles aren't.

6. *Respect the teacher.* For a good idea of how you might be perceived by a teacher, ask yourself this question: What would the teacher's life be like if every parent did what I do?

7. *Pray for the teacher.* If you multiply your needs as a parent times the teacher's twenty-five students, you will feel the need to pray for him.

JOE NEFF
Director of Guidance at Wheaton Academy
Condensed from *Focus on the Family* magazine

For Fathers

*If you take being a father seriously,
you'll know that you're not big enough for the job,
not by yourself.... Being a father will put you
on your knees if nothing else ever did.*

ELISABETH ELLIOT

*How easily a father's tenderness is recalled,
and how quickly a son's offenses vanish
at the slightest words of repentance!*

MOLIÈRE

*Fathers, do not exasperate your children;
instead, bring them up in the training
and instruction of the Lord.*

PAUL THE APOSTLE

❧

For Mothers

*The most glorious sight
that one ever sees beneath the stars
is the sight of worthy motherhood.*

GEORGE W. TRUETT

*A mother's arms are made of tenderness,
and children sleep soundly in them.*

VICTOR HUGO

*No nation ever had a better friend
than the mother who taught her
children to pray.*

AUTHOR UNKNOWN

Things Kids Hate to Hear

Can't you do anything right?

When will you ever learn?

What is wrong with you?

You are lazy.

You are stupid.

You are so immature.

Who do you think you are?

You'll be the death of me yet.

Haven't I taught you anything?

You're just no good.

You'll never amount to anything.

You got what you deserved.

You need your head examined.

Don't you care about anything?

What makes you think you're so special?

I've had it with you.

All you ever do is cause trouble.

Just wait until you have kids.

Don't you ever listen?

When are you going to start obeying me?

If I've told you once, I've told you a million times...

MIKE DeBOER
Middle school counselor

What Kids Say They Appreciate

1. We were often spontaneously hugged—even apart from completing a task or chore.

2. They would let me explain my side of the story.

3. They would take each of us out individually for a special breakfast with Mom and Dad.

4. My mother always carried pictures of each of us in her purse.

5. Mom and Dad would watch their tone of voice when they argued.

6. My parents made sure that each of us kids appeared in the family photos.

7. They were willing to admit when they were wrong and say "I'm sorry."

8. I saw my parents praying for me even when I didn't feel I deserved it.

9. My folks wrote a special "story of my birth" that they read to me every year.

10. They attended all of my open houses at school.

11. My mother and father would ask us children our opinions on important family decisions.

12. My mom had a great sense of humor, but she never made us kids the brunt of her jokes.

13. My parents wouldn't change things in my bedroom without asking me if it was okay with me.

14. When I wrecked my parents' car, my father's first reaction was to hug me and let me cry instead of yelling at me.

15. My parents were patient with me when I went through my long-hair stage in high school.

16. My mother would pray with me about important decisions I was facing, or even that I would have a good day at school.

17. We would have "family meetings" every two weeks where everyone would share their goals and problems.

18. Even though I didn't like it at the time, the chores my parents made me do helped me learn responsibility.

19. When I was down about my boyfriend breaking up with me, my father took extra time just to listen to me and cry with me.

20. My parents never acted like they were perfect, and they never expected us to be perfect either.

21. My mother would let me explain my point of view on issues—even when she disagreed with me. She always made me feel that my opinion was important.

22. My parents didn't compare my abilities with those of my older brother or the other kids at school. They helped me see my own unique value.

GARY SMALLEY AND JOHN TRENT
Selected list from *Love Is a Decision*
Selected from a list of 100

A Gift for Your Child

THE GIFT OF ATTENTION:

I will watch and listen

for your every need.

Ten Gifts for Your Teens

1. The gift of time.

2. The gift of respect.

3. The gift of hope.

4. The gift of caring for their friends.

5. The gift of parameters.

6. The gift of flexibility.

7. The gift of understanding.

8. The gift of other adult friends.

9. The gift of loving our mates.

10. The gift of a consistent role model.

SUSAN ALEXANDER YATES
Condensed from *How to Like the Ones You Love*

Kids Who Resist Peer Pressure Have . . .

An internal compass of right and wrong.

A fear of God.

General respect for parental and other authority.

A good relationship with their parents.

Self-control, including a

willingness to say no to temptations.

Self-esteem.

Self-contentment.

An unwillingness to bend the rules.

A willingness to pay the price when
they do make bad choices.

Wisdom to resist tempting environments.

DON S. OTIS
Condensed from *Teach Your Children Well*

Basics for Parenting

1. *Pay more attention to your marriage—or yourself, if you're a single parent—than you do to your children.*

   Your marriage, if it is strong and satisfying, will give your children more security than any amount of attention. If you are single, your sense of self-respect and fulfillment as a person can act as the same sort of anchor for children.

2. *Expect your children to obey.*

   Don't apologize for decisions you make in their lives. Children need powerful parents upon whom they can count to be authoritative, decisive, and trustworthy. You are in charge of the family.

3. *Nurture your children's responsibility within this structure.*

   Allow them to make choices, and let them know that they must accept the outcomes. From an early age, expect them to

make regular, tangible contributions to the family. That means chores they don't get paid for. And it means letting your children take responsibility for their own actions.

4. Say no and say it often.

If the response is a tantrum, so be it. Exposure to frustration prepares children for the realities of adulthood and gives them a tolerance of frustration that eventually develops perseverance—a key ingredient to every success story. Your obligation is not to make your children happy, but to give them the skills to pursue happiness on their own.

5. Where toys are concerned, less is more.

Having too many toys destroys a young child's ability to make creative decisions. If a youngster has too many options, he becomes overwhelmed and can't decide what to play with.

6. Turn off the tube.

Preschool children need to play so they can develop basic competency skills learned by touching and exploring their environment. Nothing happens when a child sits passively in front of a television screen.

7. Don't be intimidated by the experts.

Use suggestions and ideas that make sense to you, but remember that all parents make mistakes now and then...and children aren't permanently scarred by it. Raise your children your way and enjoy it.

JOHN ROSEMOND
Condensed from *Bottom Line Personal*

A Gift for Your Child

THE GIFT OF
COMMUNICATION:

I will take the time

to know your heart and

show you mine.

Five Steps to Better Behavior

Be consistent.

Stay cool.

Clarify the consequences.

Be forgiving.

Overlook past offenses.

GARY CHAPMAN
Condensed from *Five Signs of a Functional Family*

Pray for Your Children

1. Their health

2. Their safety

3. Their choices

4. Their temptations

5. Their contentment

6. Their faith

7. Their friends

8. Their character

9. Their future mate

10. Their legacy

DR. STEVE STEPHENS
Author and seminar speaker

13 Ways to Get Your Children to Read

1. Model reading by having everyone in the family read regularly.

2. Read to your children daily, beginning at their birth.

3. Choose early reading material carefully; make sure it is colorful, fun, and age-appropriate.

4. Show esteem for books by setting aside shelves or areas just for books.

5. Purchase some special books such as pop-up books and books autographed by authors and illustrators.

6. Buy books on tape. Better yet, have a grandparent read books onto tape.

7. Subscribe to magazines that keep children's attention and feed their interest.

8. Respect children's right to choose what to read, but also introduce books they may not read on their own.

9. Visit libraries and bookstores regularly.

10. Always have good books in the car, and take them into restaurants, offices, and other settings for "waiting times."

11. Set aside part of a child's allowance as a book purchasing fund.

12. Visit Web sites of children's authors.

13. Unplug the television.

DORIS HOWARD
Librarian

Wisdom *for* Parents

Children will remember you
not for the material things you provided but
for the feeling that you cherished them.

RICHARD I. EVANS

Affirming words from
moms and dads are like light switches.
Speak a word of affirmation at the right
moment in a child's life and it's like lighting
up a whole roomful of possibilities.

GARY SMALLEY AND JOHN TRENT

Five More Ways to Get Your Children to Read

1. Place interesting books throughout your house.

2. Give each child a small bookcase of his own.

3. Reserve several high-quality books each year for vacations or car trips.

4. Make sure books are liberally included in birthday and holiday celebrations.

5. Develop in your children a strong appreciation for the smell and feel of a new book.

BOB HOSTETLER
Condensed from "Raising Children by the Books"
HomeLife magazine

Reading Can . . .

1. Widen horizons.

2. Stimulate imaginations.

3. Counter the influence of television.

4. Encourage the discovery of new interests.

5. Strengthen family togetherness.

6. Provide a storehouse of fond memories.

BOB HOSTETLER
Condensed from "Raising Children by the Books"
HomeLife magazine

A Gift for Your Child

THE GIFT OF TEACHING:

I will tell you, in words

you can hear and understand,

the life lessons you need to know.

20 Books to Read Aloud

1. *Caddie Woodlawn* by Carol Ryrie Brink

2. The Cooper Kids adventure series by Frank Peretti

3. *The Secret Garden* by Frances Hodgson Burnett

4. The Ramona series by Beverly Cleary

5. *A Wrinkle in Time* by Madeleine L'Engle

6. The Chronicles of Narnia series by C. S. Lewis

7. *Little Women* by Louisa May Alcott

8. *House at Pooh Corner* by A. A. Milne

9. *Charlotte's Web* by E. B. White

10. *Anne of Green Gables* by L. M. Montgomery

11. *Gentle Ben* by Walt Morey

12. *The Boxcar Children* by Gertrude Chandler Warner

13. *Heidi* by Johanna Spyri

14. *Hans Brinker and the Silver Skates* by Mary Mapes Dodge

15. *The Lord of the Rings* by J. R. R. Tolkien

16. *John Bunyan's Pilgrim's Progress* by Gary D. Schmidt

17. *The Book of Virtues* by William J. Bennett

18. *The Velveteen Rabbit* by Margery Williams

19. *A Christmas Carol* by Charles Dickens

20. *Black Beauty* by Anna Sewell

JANICE BYRAM
Schoolteacher

A Gift for Your Child

THE GIFT OF PATIENCE:

*I will slow down
enough to walk beside you
and let you be you.*

Four Foundation Stones of Parental Love

1. Meeting the emotional
and nurturance needs of your child

2. Giving loving training and discipline to your child

3. Providing physical and emotional protection for your child

4. Teaching and modeling anger
management for your child

DR. ROSS CAMPBELL
From *Relational Parenting*

Affirming Your Children

PRAISE SELECTIVELY.

Indiscriminate praise doesn't motivate; it only confuses. When your child is disruptive or disrespectful, resist the myth that says they'll learn obedience by flattery. Praise only when behavior or character reflects your desires.

PRAISE IMMEDIATELY.

Delayed praise has less meaning than immediate praise. When you praise a child hours after a good choice was made, he may not remember the action. Catch your little ones "in the act" of doing something praiseworthy, and then respond immediately.

PRAISE SPECIFICALLY.

When you praise your child, assign your praise to noticeable acts or attitudes. "I like the way you shared your toy!" "What

a good job you did on making your bed today!" "Look at you. You remembered to brush your teeth all by yourself!"

PRAISE INTENTIONALLY.

Look for ways to praise your child. When your daughter brings you a finger painting, look carefully for something you like in it (maybe the colors are mostly mudlike, but notice the smudge of bright yellow). Single out what you like, and then display the piece on the refrigerator or a bulletin board. When you're going about your daily chores and you notice your toddler occupying himself with a puzzle, tell him how proud you are of his choice to play alone sometimes.

ELISA MORGAN AND CAROL KUYKENDALL
From *What Every Child Needs*

Things to Do with Your Kids

Read. Turn off the computer, the TV, and the CD or cassette player. Discover books.

Explore. Museums, historical sites, and nature locations such as parks, beaches, mountains, and—yes, caves—are great.

Invent. Cook, sew, build, invent.

Travel. Go somewhere you've never been before.

Learn. Learning new skills or improving a weak area can put your youngster ahead next year.

Play. Life is pretty serious, even for kids, so there's nothing wrong with having some fun. But do it as a family.

Work. Learning to carry out responsibility is one of the most important lessons a kid can learn.

Walk. Walking can be fun. It also gives you one-on-one time apart from the telephone, your schedule, and the noise of the TV.

Invest in others. As a family, paint an elderly widow's house or put a roof on the church. Reach out and do something for someone else.

Touch God together. Take time on that backpacking trip to focus on the beauty God has created. As you build a fire and watch the stars, listen to your kids.

HAROLD J. SALA
President of Guidelines International Ministries
Condensed from *Guidelines for Living* magazine

Family Guidelines for Using the Internet

Your kids may not be safe driving through the virtual village alone. Here are some tips to keep them from seeing the seedier side of cyberspace.

- Keep your computer in a common, visible area of the home.

- Encourage your family to telecommute together.

- Prohibit late-night Internet surfing.

- Don't allow aimless roaming. Always have a definite destination in mind.

- Decide family standards for what on-line entertainment and communication is acceptable. Explain the rules clearly and stick to them. Be sure to include these three "nevers":

1. Never give out personal information over the computer. This includes full names, addresses, phone numbers, or any financial data (credit card numbers, etc.).

2. Never respond to anyone who leaves obnoxious, lewd, or threatening e-mail.

3. Never set up a face-to-face meeting with anyone you meet via bulletin board or chat forums.

- Limit the number of minutes each family member can spend on-line.

- Periodically review file names of the documents your children download.

Condensed from *New Man* magazine

Family Guidelines for Television

1. Decide ahead of time what you want to watch.

2. Include your children when setting up guidelines.

3. Turn off the TV during meals.

4. Set a limit on how much to watch each day with a goal of decreasing your total viewing time.

5. Watch together as a couple or as a family (not alone).

6. Always do homework or chores first. (A suggested rule for every member of the family—one hour of reading before one hour of TV).

7. Set rules for baby-sitters.

8. Acquire a good collection of family videos as alternatives.

9. Pay attention to rating guides.

10. Talk about what you watch.

11. Evaluate and discuss what you see in terms of violence, language, sexual content, morality, respect for individuals, and accuracy.

12. Take advantage of viewing time together to snuggle and rub backs.

How to Get Your Kids to Help at Home

Start them young.

The younger they learn to do chores, the less resistant
they are to chores as they get older.

Teach by example.

Make sure your kids see you doing chores the way
you expect them to do chores—thoroughly and with
a positive attitude.

Provide clear instructions.

Give specific, understandable steps to complete each
chore, and then patiently demonstrate how you want
it done.

Assign what's age-appropriate.

Be aware of what's reasonable to expect at each age.
Because of coordination, strength, concentration, and

general maturity, there are some jobs that kids must "grow into."

Make it visual.

Write out job descriptions, assignment schedules, or check-off lists, and keep them posted where the kids will see them daily.

Stick with routine.

Set up certain days and times of day to do chores. Then be consistent with maintaining your routines.

Encourage teamwork.

Work together in pairs or as an entire family on certain chores. With others involved, hard tasks seem much easier and get accomplished much faster.

Reward chores well done.

Acknowledge your children's attitude and effort. Show
them your appreciation via verbal affirmation, prizes,
allowance, or special family time.

Trade chores.

Whenever possible, rotate chores among different family
members to allow for variety and to encourage all members
to learn each job.

Keep them fun.

Make chores into games or contests. Smiling, laughing, or
singing makes work seem a lot less like work. Like the old
song goes, "A spoonful of sugar helps the medicine go down."

MONICA POWERS
Creative organizer and mother of three

A Gift for Your Child

THE GIFT OF HELP:

I will assist you whenever

things become too difficult

for you to do.

Showing Respect for Your Teen

🍲 Accept your teen. Respect his developmental ability.
Don't compare him to someone else.

🍲 Allow and accept your teenager's feelings—even anger.
Remember, your teen has a right to feel his feelings.

🍲 Share your own feelings with your teen.

🍲 Don't expect more of your teen
than you do of yourself.

🍲 Show patience with problems.

~§ Discipline in private.

~§ Don't complain about your teen or about
the burdens of parenting in front of your teen.

~§ Show an interest in his friends.
Invite his friends to your house.

~§ Respect your teenager's need for privacy.

ELISA MORGAN AND CAROL KUYKENDALL
From *What Every Child Needs*

Just for Fun

- Build a "fort" with pillows and couch cushions. Wad up newspaper to make balls. Then take turns tossing the balls into the fort, with someone inside to catch the balls.

- Build a dollhouse together using boxes. Ask your child to find small objects to use as furniture.

- Read a book aloud while the rest of the family listens and paints with watercolors.

- Let your child help you make play dough by mixing one part water, one part salt, and three parts flour. Then be sculptors.

- Make "ooze dough" by mixing two parts cornstarch and one part water. See what you can do with it. Swirl different colors of food coloring into it.

- Make hand shadows on the wall by darkening the room and shining a light on your hands.

- Play some of your child's favorite recorded music, and move to the music together.

KARYN HENLEY
From *HomeLife* magazine

Minimize Materialism

- Engage in activities that don't cost much. This reinforces the principle that fun isn't always associated with money.

- Teach your children and show them by your actions that people matter more than things.

- Minimize the exposure to commercial content, including advertisements that appear in your newspaper.

- Keep conversations about major purchases or financial struggles between adults. Children don't need the added stress of knowing about or worrying over financial pressure.

- Beware of "fiction wishing." Don't say, "Wouldn't it be great if we had...?"

- Reach out to people in need by volunteering time or services. Visit those in hospitals, nursing homes, or orphanages.

- Encourage the deferral of gratification. Encourage your kids to save money in order to purchase something they want instead of just going to the store and buying it for them. Let them know they can't have everything they want and they have to make choices.

- Encourage your children to save, recycle, reuse, give away, and take care of the material items they have.

- Avoid the temptation of comparing what you or your children have with what others have.

- Explain the difference between functionality and extravagance. For example, designer clothes may not always be better.

- Reject the dress-for-success mentality.

- Talk about the fact that happiness or contentment are rarely the result of what we have. Help your children see that it is what's inside a person that counts, not how many things he or she has.

DON S. OTIS
Condensed from *Teach Your Children Well*

Wisdom for Parents

Never forget the nine most
important words of any family—

I love you.

You are beautiful.

Please forgive me.

H. JACKSON BROWN, JR.

If you can't hold children in your arms,
please hold them in your heart.

MOTHER CLARA HALE

Each day of our lives we make
deposits in the memory banks of our children.

CHARLES SWINDOLL

A Gift for Your Child

THE GIFT OF PRAYER:

I will pray for you
day and night, in both
good times and bad.

Ten Treasures for Your Children

1. *Love.* Every child wants love, and it's so easy to love a child.

2. *Discipline.* No parent likes to come home to the role of disciplinarian, yet that's exactly what your child needs from you—the strong, sure limits you provide.

3. *A good example.* The most important messages you convey to your children are the unspoken ones.

4. *Respect.* A child needs your respect in order to develop self-respect.

5. *A good self-image.* Love and respect enhance a child's self-image, but try not to overpraise or hover. Compliments for a job well done are great, but when praise is undeserved, a child knows it, and that can undermine her self-image.

6. *Good health habits.* Start early to guard his health with preventive health-care visits. Take care of yourself, too; consistently brushing your teeth, exercising, and eating healthful snacks are the surest ways to install in your child the value of taking good care of his own body.

7. *Time together.* Even though life is busy and complicated, make sure your child knows that she comes first. You need to be available to her at mealtimes, on weekends, and for school functions. Bathtime and bedtime rituals are also important, as well as sharing sports, music and fun.

8. *Motivation for learning.* All parents who are concerned about learning model that drive naturally for their children, but the danger is in pushing them beyond their limits.

9. *Sense of humor.* Laugh with your children so they can see the light and joyful side of things. Humor may not come easily when you're feeling stressed, but try not to be too serious. Laughter gives us balance.

10. *Peer relationships.* From the second year on, a child needs playmates. Through play with children his own age or slightly older, he learns about compromise and empathy; he develops new skills, interests, and responsibility to others.

T. BERRY BRAZELTON, M.D.
Condensed from *Family Circle* magazine

Home Rules

Always be honest.

Count your blessings.

Bear each other's burdens.

Forgive and forget.

Be kind and tenderhearted.

Comfort one another.

Keep your promises.

Be supportive of one another.

Be true to each other.

Look after each other.

Treat each other as you treat your friends.

But most importantly,
love one another deeply from the heart.

Selected from *The Holy Bible*

The Job of Parents

Parents can and must:

Train,

Shape,

Mold,

Correct,

Guide,

Punish,

Reward,

Instruct,

Warn,

Teach,

and Love

their kids during the formative years.

DR. JAMES C. DOBSON
From *Parenting Isn't for Cowards*

Principles of Parenting

• *Define your priorities.*

What's really important to you? Don't spin your wheels on the unimportant things—save your energy for the important issues.

• *Make your life an example for your children.*

It must be just as much "Be what I am" as it is "Do what I say." Discipline is for parents first. That is why it is so hard.

• *Study your child.*

Training your child requires studying him. Know your child. Talk with him. Ask him questions.

• *Be careful not to crush your child.*

You must never crush his will through verbal or physical intimidation. Your ultimate goal is to train him to choose right for himself, from the heart, even when you aren't around.

• *Teach your child to control himself.*

Hearing "No!" and surviving the frustration that automatically comes with it gives kids strength. It builds endurance and helps them control their frustrations and impulses.

• *Require obedience.*

Say yes whenever you possibly can. But when you say no, mean it. If you must discipline, make the pain of the discipline outweigh the pleasure of disobedience, or it will be meaningless to your child.

• *Teach respect for other people and for property.*

Respect starts in the home. By learning respect at a young age, kids see that people and things should not be targets for their wrath.

• *Teach hard work.*

From a very early age, a child should be a helping member of the family unit. This requires patient, creative, structured teaching. First you do it for him; then you do it together; finally, he does it himself.

• *Give many rewards.*

Punishment teaches what not to do. You want to teach your child that good and pleasure go together just as surely as sin and pain. Reward kindness, good deeds, and cheerful obedience.

• *Forget guilt trips.*

We all make mistakes, children and parents alike. Children would rather live with a parent who makes an occasional mistake than with one who never cares enough to discipline them at all.

JANI ORTLUND
Condensed from *Fearlessly Feminine*

A Gift for Your Child

THE GIFT OF DISCIPLINE:

I will correct you firmly

and consistently and lovingly

whenever the need arises.

Wisdom for Parents

For Fathers

*Let every father remember that
one day his son will follow his example
instead of his advice.*

AUTHOR UNKNOWN

Dad

*He dreams, he plans,
He struggles that we might have the best.
His sacrifice is quiet, his life is love expressed.*

AUTHOR UNKNOWN

*The most important thing a father
can do for his children is to love their mother.*

THEODORE M. HESBURGH

Wisdom *for* Parents

For Mothers

The heart of a mother is
a deep abyss at the bottom of which
you will always find forgiveness.

HONORÉ DE BALZAC

Before becoming a mother I had
a hundred theories on how to bring up children.
Now I have seven children and only one theory:
Love them, especially when they least deserve to be loved.

KATE SAMPERI

A rich child often sits
in a poor mother's lap.

DANISH PROVERB

Five Secrets of Parenting Teens

1. *Care about What Matters to Them*

All teenagers need the assurance that you have taken notice
of their lives, that you have made a special effort to take
interest in the things that matter to them. Make their interests
your interests.

2. *Embrace Moments of Personal Pain*

Most of the time, heartbreak in a teenager's life seems trite to
us. But when painful times hit, it's an open door for you to
build trust and respect with your teenager.

3. *Prepare to Be Taken for Granted—It Is Well Worth It*

The task of making boys and girls into men and women is
not for the feeble at heart. Accept the fact that raising kids

means long days and sleepless nights with rare instances of gratitude.

4. *Stay Steady*

More than anything else, teenagers are looking for people who will go the distance with them. They need you to pass the test of time and be there.

5. *Practice Modeling*

Whether we realize it or not, our kids are modeling their lives after ours. Count on it—they take note of everything we do and everything we say.

TED HAGGARD AND JOHN BOLIN
From *Confident Parents, Exceptional Teens*

Teambuilding

1. Great Goals—Promote activities in which siblings must work together to reach a goal.

2. Games—During family time, join the children as a team.

3. Working Together—Assign chores that must be completed with cooperation.

4. Charity Work—Unite your children to reach out to the less fortunate.

5. Fun Projects—Promote sibling activities such as large puzzles, birdhouses, or craft kits to develop a sense of teamwork. Use limited supplies such as glue and markers so children will have to share.

6. An Offering for Every Occasion—Unite forces to create gifts, such as cookies, for neighbors or grandparents.

7. Book Time—Have children read to each other, or have an older child read to a younger sibling. Also, make up your own "sibling"

stories for your children. Have Super Brother save little sister from the scary bear, or add your children as characters to Bible stories.

8. *King or Queen for the Day*—Make one day a week "Royal Kid Day." One child is designated king or queen for the day to receive special treatment. The other "servant" children also enjoy themselves as they prepare food and games for the queen or king.

9. *Special Parent Day*—Siblings will have tons of fun working together to fulfill the needs of the chosen adult. (This is great for the adults, too!)

10. *Family Talent Night*—Encourage each child to shine like a star in front of the family. Tumbling acts, singing specials, or the presentation of school projects will bring applause and support from other siblings.

TRICIA GOYER AND CINDY McCORMICK MARTINUSEN
Condensed from *HomeLife* magazine

How to Choose a Video for Your Family

1. *Check the rating.* "Unrated" means unknown. You have no idea what you are getting. If the video is rated, you'll find it on the back side of the jacket box. "G" means the movie is suitable for all audiences. "PG" means parental guidance is suggested. "PG-13" often contains significant doses of sex and violence. "R" means restricted, with no one under seventeen allowed to watch without a parent or adult guardian.

2. *Ask the right questions.* Even when a rating is displayed on the box, discernment is crucial in choosing a videocassette. The following questions will help you:

* What is the premise of the movie? What message does the film communicate? You can often find the premise on the jacket of the videotape. Remember: You have to read between the lines.

- Who is the hero and what kind of role model is he?

- How is religion portrayed?

- How is the world portrayed?

- How is love portrayed?

- How is the family portrayed?

3. *Know what you want to rent before you walk into the store.*
If you do find yourself browsing, head for the "classics" or "musicals"
sections. They stand a better chance of being good for family viewing.

4. *Totally avoid horror movies and teen sexploitation films.*

TED BAEHR
Condensed from *The War Cry* magazine

20 Great Children's Movies

(for ages six and older)

1. Adventures of Milo and Otis

2. Anne of Green Gables

3. Babe

4. Beauty and the Beast

5. Benji

6. The Black Stallion

7. A Bug's Life

8. Pippi Longstocking

9. Homeward Bound

10. Lady and the Tramp

11. Mary Poppins

12. Miracle on 34th Street

13. Chicken Run

14. Oliver and Company

15. Pinocchio

16. Pollyanna

17. Prince of Egypt

18. Toy Story (I and II)

19. The Tigger Movie

20. Rugrats in Paris: The Movie

JOHN EVANS
Editor-in-chief, *Preview Family Movie and TV Review*

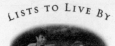

20 Great Family Movies

(for ages twelve and older)

1. Anna and the King (1999)

2. Chariots of Fire

3. Christy

4. Driving Miss Daisy

5. The Santa Clause

6. Sabrina (1995)

7. Small Wonders

8. Inn of the Sixth Happiness

9. It's a Wonderful Life

10. Little Women (1994)

11. Mr. Smith Goes to Washington

12. Life Is Beautiful

13. The Quiet Man

14. The Preacher's Wife (1996)

15. The Sound of Music

16. Stuart Little

17. Winslow Boy

18. To Kill a Mockingbird

19. Remember the Titans

20. Angels in the Outfield

JOHN EVANS

Editor-in-chief, *Preview Family Movie and TV Review*

50 Ways to Love Your Children

1. Hug them every morning.

2. Go to zoos, parades, and amusement parks.

3. Hang their art and awards on the refrigerator.

4. Create family traditions.

5. Be patient.

6. Apologize when grumpy.

7. Go camping.

8. Play tic-tac-toe and hide 'n' seek.

9. Always carry Band-Aids and gumdrops.

10. Know their strengths.

11. Compliment them.

12. Encourage them.

13. Appreciate them.

14. Eat meals together.

15. Slow down.

16. Respect their privacy.

17. Listen.

18. Don't discipline in anger.

19. Be consistent.

20. Say "I love you" frequently.

21. Let them be silly.

22. Accept imperfections.

23. Reward good behavior.

24. Explain the rules clearly.

25. Laugh often.

26. Go to their favorite restaurants.

27. Invite their friends over.

28. Buy ice cream cones.

29. Go on vacations.

30. Know when to be gentle and when to be firm.

31. Make birthdays unforgettable.

32. Teach responsibility and respect.

33. Choose your battles.

34. Don't embarrass them.

35. Help with schoolwork.

36. Protect them.

37. Build memories.

38. Keep promises.

39. Say "no" when needed.

40. Don't yell.

41. Give gifts.

42. Model virtues.

43. Pray with them.

44. Pray for them.

45. Talk with their teachers.

46. Tell them you're proud of them.

47. Reach out.

48. Count stars together.

49. Talk every bedtime.

50. Let go with a blessing.

DR. STEVE STEPHENS
From *Stories for the Family's Heart*

A Father's Love

Fathers are kind,

Fathers are nice,

They give you hugs and kisses right before bed.

They love you through all the days of your life.

BRITTANY STEPHENS
Age 8

❧

At the end only two things really matter...
and they are the affection and understanding
of [one's] family. Anything and everything else...
is insubstantial.

RICHARD E. BYRD

Live your life so that when you're old,
people will know that you
—loved others clearly
—loved your family dearly
—loved God completely.

BRUCE AND STAN

Help for Hurting Parents

1. You are not to blame for the temperament with which your child was born. He is simply a tough kid to handle, and your task is to rise to the challenge.

2. He is in greater danger because of his inclination to test the limits and scale the walls. Your utmost diligence and wisdom will be required to deal with him.

3. If you fail to understand his lust for power and independence, you can exhaust your resources and become bogged down in guilt.

4. If it is not already too late, by all means, take charge of your babies. Hold tightly to the reins of authority in the early days, and build an attitude of respect during your brief window of opportunity. You will need every ounce of "awe" you can get during the years to come. Once you have established your right to lead, begin to let go systematically, year by year.

5. Don't panic, even during the storms of your child's adolescence. Better times are ahead. A radical turnaround usually occurs in the early twenties.

6. Stay on your child's team, even when it appears to be a losing team. You'll have the rest of your life to enjoy mutual fellowship if you don't overreact to frustration now.

7. Give your child time to find himself, even if he appears not to be searching.

8. Most importantly, I urge you to hold your children before the Lord in fervent prayer throughout their years at home. I am convinced that there is no greater source of confidence and wisdom in parenting.

DR. JAMES C. DOBSON
From *Parenting Isn't for Cowards*

A Gift for Your Child

THE GIFT OF DIRECTION:

*I will show you a
positive path to go and a
positive way to walk it.*

A Parent's Commitment

- We are committed to help our children be successful in whatever they want to do.

- We will be committed to them after they are married.

- We will be committed to them no matter whom they marry.

- We will be committed to them no matter what happens during their marriage.

- We will be committed to their mates and to their children.

- We will always be available to listen.

- Should they get into trouble, we will be there to help.

GARY SMALLEY AND JOHN TRENT
From *Leaving the Light On*

Ten Family Commitments

1. I will not hit.

2. I will not keep secrets.

3. I will not lie.

4. I will not use bad language.

5. I will not use drugs, and if I know somebody who is using drugs, I'll try to help them.

6. I will treat others with respect.

7. If I make a mess, I'll clean it up.

8. I'll pick up my clothes and keep my room neat.

9. I'll talk to Mom and Dad about my problems.

10. I'll do my homework before I go out to play.

GREG CYNAUMON, PH.D.
From *How to Avoid Alienating Your Kids*

Messages for Your Baby

"I belong."
Those hours in your arms give your baby
the message, "I am loved. Somebody's there for me."

"I'm special."
It is never too early to begin affirming
your baby and letting him know how valuable
he is in God's eyes and in your heart.

"I trust."
Because in his distress you comfort him, your baby learns...
that you will respond and are worthy of his trust.

"I can."
Applaud your baby's milestones. Show your
joy as he stretches his little body and his mind.

WILLIAM SEARS, MARTHA SEARS, JOYCE WARMAN, ET AL.
From *Parent Project: Tools for Godly Parenting*

Bolstering Your Child's Confidence

Notice and affirm when he does well.

"Your words showed understanding. I'm proud of the way you cared for your friend."

Find strengths related to every weakness.

"You ran hard after that soccer ball" rather than "Why can't you learn how to kick the ball properly?"

Downplay criticism. When you have to criticize, focus on the action rather than the child.

"Being late makes it hard to trust you" rather than "You're always late! I'll never be able to trust you again!"

Point out something positive about frustrations.

"Even though you were late, you did call. That shows consideration and a sense of responsibility."

Help children solve their own problems.

"How might we master this lateness problem? I know it's as frustrating for you as it is for me." Together with your child, list several possibilities and agree to implement one.

Guide your children to evaluate their actions.

"What went well in your plan? What might we have done even better? What action would you change if you could do it again?"

KAREN DOCKREY
From *Parenting: Questions Women Ask*

25 Ways to Enjoy Your Family

1. Eat dinner together as a family for seven days in a row.

2. Take your spouse on a dialogue date.

3. Read your kids a classic book.

4. Memorize the Twenty-third Psalm as a family.

5. Give each family member a hug for twenty-one days in a row (that's how long the experts say it takes to develop a habit).

6. Pick three nights of the week on which the television will remain off.

7. Pray for your spouse and children every day.

8. Plan a vacation together.

9. Take a vacation together.

10. Sit together as a family in church.

11. Take a few hours one afternoon and go to the library as a family.

12. Write each member of your family a letter sharing why you value them.

13. Take each of your children out to breakfast (individually) at least once a month for a year.

14. Help your kids with their homework.

15. Put together a picture puzzle (Five hundred pieces or more).

16. Encourage each child to submit to you his most perplexing question, and promise that you'll either answer it or discuss it with him.

17. Tell your kids how you and your spouse met.

18. Call your spouse from work just to see how he or she is doing.

19. Compile a family tree and tell your children about their ancestors.

20. Get involved in a family project that serves or helps someone less fortunate.

21. Spend an evening going through old pictures from family vacations.

22. Praise your spouse and children—in their presence—to someone else.

23. Declutter your house.

24. Become a monthly supporter of a Third World child.

25. Give each child the freedom to pick his favorite dinner menu at least once a month.

TIM KIMMEL
Selected from *Little House on the Freeway*

A Gift for Your Child

THE GIFT OF ENCOURAGEMENT:

I will believe the best in you,

complimenting and praising you

every chance I get.

How Well Do You Know Your Teenager?

Who is your teen's best friend?

What color would she like for the walls in her bedroom?

Who is your teen's greatest hero?

What embarrasses your teen the most?

What is your teen's biggest fear?

What is his favorite type of music?

What person outside the immediate family has most influenced your teen?

What is his favorite school subject?

What is her least favorite school subject?

What has your teen done that he feels most proud of?

What is your teen's biggest complaint about the family?

What sport does your teen most enjoy?

What is her favorite TV program?

What makes your teen especially angry?

What would your teen like to be when he grows up?

What chore does your teen like least?

What three foods does your teen like most?

What is your teen's most prized possession?

What is her favorite family occasion?

What activity did your teen enjoy most last weekend?

MIRIAM NEFF, M.A.
High school counselor
Condensed from *FamilyLife Today* magazine

Ten Important Manners to Teach Your Children

1. Meeting and greeting people properly.

2. Being a gracious host and a welcome guest.

3. Good speaking manners: "Yes" and "no"
(or "Yes ma'am" and "No ma'am," not "yeah" or a grunt),
"hello," "good-bye," "thank you," "please,"
"excuse me," "I'm sorry," and "may I?"

4. Proper conduct for church and other public places.

5. Writing, coloring, or drawing thank-you notes.

6. Properly responding to invitations and following through on response.

7. Good (not perfect) table manners.

8. Proper telephone talk.

9. Showing deference to elders and authority figures.

10. Opening doors for others.

JUNE MOORE
Moore Than Manners Consulting

The Bottom Line

꿍 When your children ask "Who's in charge?" tell them.

꿍 When they mutter "Who loves me?" take them in your arms and surround them with affection.

꿍 When they defiantly challenge you, win decisively. Talk to them. Set up clear boundaries and then enforce the rules firmly and fairly.

꿍 Expose your children to interesting things. Help them use their time wisely.

꿍 Raise them in a stable family with two parents who love each other and enjoy a strong marriage.

༚ Teach them to love the Lord and understand His Word.

༚ Treat them with respect and dignity and expect the same in return.

༚ Set aside time to build friendship and love between generations.

DR. JAMES AND SHIRLEY DOBSON
From *Night Light*

Ten Ways to Be a Great Dad

1. Respect your children's mother.

One of the best things a father can do for his children is to respect their mother. If you are married, keep your marriage strong and vital. If you're not married, it is still important to respect and support the mother of your children.

2. Spend time with your children.

How a father spends his time tells his children what's important to him. If you always seem too busy for your children, they will feel neglected no matter what you say.

3. Earn the right to be heard.

All too often the only time a father speaks to his children is when they have done something wrong. Begin talking with your kids when they are very young so that difficult subjects will be

easier to handle as they get older. Take time to listen to their ideas and problems.

4. Discipline with love.

All children need guidance and discipline, not as punishment but to set reasonable limits. Remind your children of the consequences of their actions, and provide meaningful rewards for desirable behavior.

5. Be a role model.

Fathers are role models to their kids whether they realize it or not. A girl who spends time with a loving father grows up knowing she deserves to be treated with respect by boys and what to look for in a husband. Fathers can teach sons what is important in life by demonstrating honesty, humility, and responsibility.

6. Be a teacher.

Too many fathers think teaching is something others do. But a father who teaches his children about right and wrong and encourages them to do their best will see his children make good choices.

7. Eat together as a family.

Sharing a meal together (breakfast, lunch, or dinner) can be an important part of healthy family life. In addition to providing some structure in a busy day, it gives kids the chance to talk about what they are doing and want to do.

8. Read to your children.

Begin reading to your children when they are very young. When they are older, encourage them to read on their own. Instilling in your children a love for reading is one of the best ways to ensure they will have a lifetime of personal and career growth.

9. Show affection.

Children need security that comes from knowing they are wanted, accepted, and loved by their family. Parents, especially fathers, need to feel both comfortable and willing to hug their children. Showing affection every day is the best way to let your children know you love them.

10. Realize that a father's job is never done.

Even after children are grown and ready to leave home, they will still look to their fathers for wisdom and advice. Whether it's continued schooling, a new job, or a wedding, fathers continue to play an essential part in the lives of their children as they grow and, perhaps, marry and build their own families.

THE NATIONAL FATHERHOOD INITIATIVE

A Gift for Your Child

THE GIFT OF EXAMPLE:

I will be a model
of virtue and character.

Eight Foundation Builders for Your Family

1. Hug and praise them.

2. See discipline as an asset.

3. Create traditions.

4. Cultivate laughter.

5. Stay close to teachers.

6. Be where they are.

7. Share your life with them.

8. Keep a long-range perspective.

SUSAN ALEXANDER YATES
From *How to Like the Ones You Love*

❧

For Fathers

The heart of every child
beats to the rhythm of a father's love.

STEVE CURLEY

His heritage to his children wasn't words or possessions,
but an unspoken treasure, the treasure of his example
as a man and a father. More than anything I have,
I'm trying to pass that on to my children.

WILL ROGERS JR.

One father is worth more
than a hundred schoolmasters.

ENGLISH PROVERB

For Mothers

No man is poor who has a godly mother.

ABRAHAM LINCOLN

*Nothing can compare in beauty, and wonder,
and admirableness, and divinity itself, to the silent
work in obscure dwellings of faithful women
bringing their children to honor and virtue and piety.*

HENRY WARD BEECHER

*If love is sweet as a flower,
then my mother is that sweet flower of love.*

STEVIE WONDER

A Child's Ten Commandments to Parents

Commandment 1: My hands are small; please don't expect perfection whenever I make a bed, draw a picture, or throw a ball. My legs are short; please slow down so I can keep up with you.

Commandment 2: My eyes have not seen the world as yours have; please let me explore safely. But don't restrict me unnecessarily.

Commandment 3: Housework will always be there. I'm only little for such a short time—please take time to explain things to me about this wonderful world, and do so willingly.

Commandment 4: My feelings are tender; please be sensitive to my needs. Don't nag me all day long. (You wouldn't want to be nagged for your inquisitiveness.) Treat me as you would like to be treated.

Commandment 5: I am a special gift from God; please treasure me as God intended you to do, holding me accountable for my actions, giving me guidelines to live by, and disciplining me in a loving manner.

Commandment 6: I need your encouragement, but not your praise, to grow. Please go easy on the criticism; remember, you can criticize the things I do without criticizing me.

Commandment 7: Please give me the freedom to make decisions concerning myself. Permit me to fail so that I can learn from my mistakes. Then someday I'll be prepared to make the kinds of decisions life requires of me.

Commandment 8: Please don't do things over for me. Somehow that makes me feel that my efforts didn't quite measure up to your expectations. I know it's hard, but please try not to compare me to my brother or my sister.

Commandment 9: Please don't be afraid to leave for a weekend together. Kids need vacations from parents, just as parents need vacations from kids. Besides, it's a great way to show us kids that your marriage is very special.

Commandment 10: Please take me to Sunday school and church regularly, setting a good example for me to follow. I enjoy learning more about God.

DR. KEVIN LEMAN
From *Getting the Best Out of Your Kids*

A Gift for Your Child

THE GIFT OF FAITH:

I will plant in you a picture
of a loving God who sees all, hears all,
knows all, and can do all.

Teaching the ABC's to Your Children

Always be on time.

Be a model of honesty.

Care about their hurts.

Do acts of kindness.

Every day, give plenty of hugs and kisses.

Forget past offenses.

Give occasional "token gifts" of love.

Have a happy disposition—"a merry heart."

Invest quality time.

Jump for joy when they bring home a good grade.

Keep looking for the good and positive.

Listen to their cares and woes and excitement.

Make adjustments for physical pain.

Never criticize in front of their peers.

Only say words that edify, that they may want to live up to them.

Put on the heart of patience.

Quietly discipline in private.

Recognize that each child is creatively, uniquely different and specially gifted.

Spend time reading to them and listening to them read.

Take care of yourself.

Understand the age-appropriate behavior of each child.

Voice—teach them to share facts, thoughts, ideas, dreams, opinions, intuition.

Welcome their friends.

X-ray to the needs of the heart.

Yesterday doesn't have to dictate today.

Zoom in on good behavior.

GLENDA HOTTON, M.A.
Counselor

Helping Your Children Succeed

Help children choose their own goals.

Help children visualize the positive results of
achieving their own goals and the negative
results of not reaching their goals.

Remember the power of praise.

Expose children to a variety of activities.

Expect children to do things right.

Believe that your children can achieve great things.

Help children develop a more positive self-image.

Reward your children.

Use the ol' "You can do it, can't you?" principle.

Be persistent.

Be enthusiastic.

Develop strong inner convictions.

GARY SMALLEY
From *The Key to Your Child's Heart*

20 Fun Activities

1. Bake cookies.

2. Help a neighbor.

3. Enjoy nature (e.g., watch for animals, set up a bird feeder, get an ant farm, collect bugs, find shapes in the clouds, study the stars).

4. Visit a zoo or museum or carnival.

5. Create a painting or a poster.

6. Put on a play or puppet show.

7. Find something to collect (shells, coins, rocks, sports cards, anything).

8. Plant a garden.

9. Collect cans and bottles, and give the money to charity.

10. Fly a kite.

11. Take flowers and a card to someone sick or lonely.

12. Read books aloud.

13. Make giant pictures on your driveway with sidewalk chalk.

14. Do a talent show.

15. Go on a hike or bicycle ride.

16. Look at family photographs or videos.

17. Tell stories.

18. Make family cards for Christmas, Valentine's Day, Thanksgiving, and birthdays.

19. Paint each other's faces.

20. Sing songs and/or make up songs.

TAMI STEPHENS
Mother of three

20 Favorite Sing-Along Songs

1. Old McDonald Had a Farm

2. She'll Be Coming 'round the Mountain

3. Row, Row, Row Your Boat

4. Oh, Susannah

5. Bingo

6. I've Been Working on the Railroad

7. If You're Happy and You Know It

8. This Old Man

9. Twinkle, Twinkle Little Star

10. On Top of Old Smokey

11. Take Me out to the Ballgame

12. Jesus Loves the Little Children

13. Mary Had a Little Lamb

14. Itsy-Bitsy Spider

15. London Bridge Is Falling Down

16. It's Raining, It's Pouring

17. Clementine

18. The Old Grey Mare

19. Are You Sleeping?

20. Ring around the Rosies

DEBRA CROCKETT
Music teacher

A Gift for Your Child

THE GIFT OF DREAMS:

I will help you to develop good

dreams and teach you what it takes to

successfully reach beyond the stars.

Ten Essential Toys

1. Puzzles

Fun for any age. They can provide hours of entertainment while teaching patience and logic.

2. A Costume Trunk

Include clothespins and safety pins with discarded outfits to customize the fit. You can get all sort of shoes and dress-up clothes at garage sales and thrift shops.

3. A Craft Box

Crayons, markers, scissors, stickers, glue sticks, string, and plenty of paper. Leave the kids alone and let their creativity bloom.

4. Cardboard Boxes

From shoe boxes to refrigerator boxes, it's amazing what kids can do with boxes. The greater the variety and number of

boxes, the better. Add duct tape to join boxes and markers to decorate them.

5. Legos

Kids love these tiny plastic squares. They can build and create almost anything with them—cars, rocket ships, castles, houses, or entire cities. Remember, Legos aren't just for boys.

6. Balls

You can kick them, throw them, shoot them, roll them, or even sit on them. Get as many sizes and styles as you can. Your kids will play with these from toddlerhood through adulthood.

7. Dolls

Give your daughters clothes to change them, bottles to feed them, and blankets to keep them warm. Use a box with a pillow and a towel for a bassinet.

8. Puppets

Help your kids make their own hand puppets out of socks or papier-mâché. Use a table with a blanket over it as a stage. Then let the show begin!

9. Bug Jar and Magnifying Glass

Go on a bug search and examine what you find with the magnifying glass. Teach your kids to safely scoop up the critters and seal them in a clear plastic jar. Watch them for a few hours, and then let them go.

10. Play Money and a Toy Cash Register

Play store and stock it with empty food boxes and cans. Provide a pen and stickers for pricing. Then take turns being the cashier and the customer.

MONICA POWERS
Mother of three

20 Games for Every Home

1. Candyland

2. Chutes and Ladders

3. Sorry

4. Pictionary

5. Concentration

6. Checkers

7. Chess

8. Dominoes

9. Chinese Checkers

10. Scrabble

11. Scattergories

12. Boggle

13. Payday

14. Life

15. Yahtzee

16. Cribbage

17. Jenga

18. Uno

19. Old Maid

20. Monopoly

TAMI STEPHENS
Mother of three

The Six A's of Parenting

1. Be aware.

Study your children. They're wonderful creations. Listen to them; watch them; ask them questions. Talk with them, not *at* them. Discover their likes and dislikes, their dreams and fears, their strengths and weaknesses. Recognize how special they are.

2. Be assertive.

There are lessons you've learned from life, so pass them on. Teach truth. Provide reasonable rules and consistent consequences when those rules are broken. Be strong; give your children security without being rigid, insensitive, abusive, angry, or exasperating.

3. Be accepting.

Focus on the positives, and assist your children with their negatives. Don't expect perfection, lest they turn and expect it from you. Remember that children are often immature, and teenagers are frequently impulsive. Be patient with them.

4. Be approachable.

One of the biggest parental problems is emotional distance from one's children. Be close to them. Spend quality time with them. Laugh with them; play with them; enjoy them. Take them on walks and outings and vacations. Truly connect with them.

5. Be affectionate.

Hug them often and tell them you love them every day. Give them compliments, and encourage instead of discouraging them. Don't yell, hit, name-call, or belittle. Treat them gently and with respect. Treasure them.

6. Be alert.

The world is full of dangers and temptations. As parents, you are protectors. Watch over your children and warn them. Protect them without being paranoid. Most importantly, pray for them daily.

20 Conversation Starters

- Tell me about the neatest birthday present you ever received.

- What makes you laugh?

- Where would you like to go for a vacation if you could go anyplace in the world?

- If you had to move and could take only three things with you, what would you take?

- Describe the "ideal" father.

- What is something you can do pretty well?

- What is your favorite song?

- What is your best friend like?

- How would you describe yourself to someone who does not know you?

- Tell about a time when you felt proud of yourself.

- What kind of store would you like to own and operate?

- If you received five thousand dollars as a gift, how would you spend it?

- What is your favorite room in your house? Why?

- What kind of job do you want to have in twenty years?

- What talent do you wish you had?

- What is your favorite food?

- If someone could give you anything in the world for your birthday, what would you like it to be?

- What would you like to invent to make life better?

- What is something that "bugs" you?

- What kind of trophy would you like to win?

JERRY AND PATTI MACGREGOR

From *Family Times: Growing Together in Fun and Faith*

How to Raise Sexually Pure Kids

Love them.

Provide them two loving role models.

Teach them who they are.

Teach them moral values.

Keep them active in church.

Help them select their friends.

Warn them about the joys and dangers of sex.

Provide them with clear guidelines for dating.

Teach them moral boundaries.

Help them make a formal commitment to virtue.

Teach them to purify their minds.

Teach them how to say "No."

Watch for signs of sexual involvement.

Provide good reading material that supports your values.

Surround them with prayer.

TIM AND BEVERLY LaHAYE
Adapted from *Raising Sexually Pure Kids*

Warning Signs That Your Child Is Headed for Trouble

Your child may be headed for trouble if he or she...

becomes lonely, quiet, or moody.

seems depressed.

has very low self-esteem.

begins having difficulty sleeping.

seems negative about everything.

begins to isolate himself.

is often angry and abusive.

becomes argumentative and lies to you.

begins fighting at school and at home.

lets his school grades fall.

changes her eating habits.

begins violating curfew times.

is arrested for shoplifting.

drops out of once-loved activities.

gets caught drinking or taking drugs.

refuses to go to church anymore.

becomes lazy and procrastinates regularly.

dates or befriends kids against your wishes.

becomes sexually active.

makes a sudden, dramatic change in his appearance.

stops making eye contact.

DR. GREG CYNAUMON
Adapted from *Helping Single Parents with Troubled Kids*

How to Free Up More Time . . .

. . . upon the arrival of a new baby

Embrace routines. Establish a daily and weekly routine for household chores.

Accept help. Hire whatever outside help you can afford during your baby's early months.

Get organized. Make lists: Determine and prioritize what tasks need to be done each day, week, or month. Condense errands into a single shopping trip.

Learn to juggle. Never tackle anything while your baby is sleeping that can be done when he is awake.

Just say no. If you try to do it all, you'll get stressed out and your whole family will lose.

Reduce clutter. If you're not using certain toys, clothes, or other items, give them to local charities or take them to resale shops.

Go barefoot. Take your shoes off by the door. It keeps carpets cleaner and means less vacuuming and carpet cleaning.

Divide and conquer. When faced with a large job, eliminate interruptions by having one parent take the baby out for a while rather than lend a hand with the task.

Be sociable. Share weekly jobs with a friend—one week at her house, the next week at yours. You'll cut work in half and have a chance to visit with another parent.

REBECCA SWEAT
Condensed from *Christian Parenting Today* magazine

The Seven Vital Needs of Young Children

1. Ongoing nurturing relationships

Every baby needs a warm, intimate relationship with a primary caregiver over a period of years, not months or weeks.

2. Physical protection, safety, and regulation

Both in the womb and in infancy, children need an environment that provides protection from physical and psychological harm, chemical toxins, and exposure to violence.

3. Experiences tailored to individual differences

Every child has a unique temperament. Tailoring early experiences to nurture a child's individual nature prevents learning and behavioral problems and enables a child to develop to his or her full potential.

4. Developmentally appropriate experiences

Children of different ages need care tailored to their individual stages. Unrealistic expectations can hinder a child's development.

5. Limit-setting, structure, and expectations

Children need structure and discipline. They need adults who empathize as well as set limits. They need expectations rather than labels and adults who believe in their potential but understand their weaknesses. They need incentive systems, not failure models.

6. Stable, supportive communities and culture

To feel whole and integrated, children need to grow up in a stable community. This means a continuity of values in family, peer groups, religion, and culture, as well as exposure to diversity.

7. Protection for the future

Meeting all these needs should be our highest priority. If we fail, we will jeopardize our children's futures.

T. BERRY BRAZELTON AND STANLEY GREENSPAN
Condensed from *The Irreducible Needs of Children*

Three Ways to Keep Family Boundaries

1. Simplify the rules.

Begin by prioritizing what's essential to you and your family:
Everyone is kind to one another, everyone puts dirty clothes in
the hamper, everyone takes turns helping in the kitchen. By
eliminating the rules that don't matter, you'll have more energy
to follow through on those that do.

2. Enforce safety and health rules and don't compromise.

Everyone washes up before dinner, everyone wears a seatbelt in
the car, everyone puts his or her toys away when finished playing.

3. Be consistent.

If you make a rule, stick with it whether it's over the weekend or
on the busiest day of your week. Your kids will appreciate the
boundaries, and their behavior will reflect it in the long run.

MARY MANZ SIMON
Condensed from *Christian Parenting Today* magazine

Seven Principles of Discipline

1. Establish a healthy authority over your children.

2. Hold your children accountable for their actions.

3. Let reality be the teacher.

4. Use action more than words.

5. Stick to your guns, but don't shoot yourself in the foot.

6. Relationships come before rules.

7. Live by your values.

DR. KEVIN LEMAN
Adapted from *Making Children Mind without Losing Yours*

Giving Love to Children

Give the choice of love.

Commit to love because it is right, not because it feels good.

Give the words of love.

We all need regular verbal assurance, but children need it the most.

Give the touch of love.

Research has confirmed the human need for physical touch. The need to be held and cuddled is especially critical for babies.

Give the encouragement of love.

Put courage "into" those little people by letting them know that you are their biggest fan and cheerleader.

Give the comfort of love.

In times of pain or sadness, love offers healing comfort.

Give the laughter of love.

Laughter sets a pleasant mood, a bright tone. Make merriment a daily dose of love in your home.

Give the discipline of love.

Discipline establishes boundaries for children, making them feel safe and secure.

DONNA OTTO
From *The Gentle Art of Mentoring*

Wisdom for Parents

Home should be a retreat to which children
can return in triumph or defeat, in victory
or disgrace, and know they are loved.

AUTHOR UNKNOWN

Children need models rather than critics.

JOSEPH JOUBERT

I have no greater joy than to hear
that my children are walking in the truth.

JOHN THE APOSTLE

Priceless Gifts

The most priceless gifts to give our children are...

1.

LIFE

2.

LOVE

3.

LAUGHTER

PHYLLIS DRYDEN
Poet and critic

Eight Ways to Practice Humor

1. Keep a journal of ridiculous things that happen to your family.

2. Buy goofy joke books.

3. Encourage your kids to cut out and share their favorite newspaper comics.

4. White out the captions of cartoons, and have your kids write their own.

5. When you're under stress, look for the lighter side.

6. Develop a playful reaction to a problem.

7. Point out verbal humor like puns and oxymorons.

8. Keep a "lighten up" prop, like fake glasses and a nose, to don when things get tense.

FAITH TIBBETTS MCDONALD
Condensed from *Christian Parenting Today* magazine

Helping Your Children Get to Sleep

1. *Be consistent.*

   Set a regular bedtime, and try to hit it as often as possible.

2. *Don't allow them to get overtired.*

   The more overtired they are, the harder it will be for them to sleep.

3. *Make their rooms comfortable.*

   Provide them with sleepable beds and peaceful rooms with the right temperature and lighting.

4. *Don't send them to their room as discipline.*

   If they are sent to their room when in trouble, they might associate being sent to bed as a form of punishment.

5. *Develop calming activities.*

   Use these during the hour before bedtime to settle them down.

6. *Establish bedtime rituals.*

Consistent patterns—brushing teeth, telling bedtime stories, laying beside them, and saying prayers—help prepare them for sleep.

7. *Play music.*

Play music your children find calm, gentle and relaxing. Play it nightly as they drift to sleep.

8. *Be calm but firm.*

Don't be manipulated about bedtime. Realize that if you become loud or upset, they will have a harder time getting to sleep.

Prepare Them for the Unexpected

1. Help your kids expect the unexpected.

The advent of the unexpected is not the end of the world.

2. Portray the unexpected as an opportunity rather than a disaster.

How you personally respond to the unexpected will have a
powerful impact on how your kids respond.

*3. Tell your kids how other people have met unexpected challenges
and gotten through them.*

This dynamic characterizes every true hero. This is the
power of stories—classic stories, stories about true sports
heroes, stories about your parents, stories from your
own experience.

4. Remind them to stick to the fundamentals of the game plan and not to panic.

Stay steady, and they will come through.

RICKY BYRDSONG

Condensed from *Coaching Your Kids in the Game of Life*

Wisdom *for* Parents

*There are many ways to
measure success, not the least of which is
the way your child describes you
when talking to a friend.*

AUTHOR UNKNOWN

*As the family goes,
so goes the nation,
and so goes the whole world
in which we live.*

JOHN PAUL II

How to Let Go

1. Your child is not the legitimate center of life
(he is profoundly instructive, satisfying,
and pleasurable, but temporary).

2. Transition is easier when
the job of child-rearing is done well.

3. An adult child is responsible for his
own decisions—you cannot make them for him.

HOWARD AND JEANNE HENDRICKS
Condensed from *Kindred Spirit* magazine

Wisdom *for* Parents

❧

Train a child

in the way he should go,

and when he is old he will

not depart from it.

KING SOLOMON

Lists for Our Family

Promises we want to make for the future...

_____

_____

_____

_____

_____

_____

_____

_____

_____

_____

Lists for Our Family

How to help one another succeed…

_____

_____

_____

_____

_____

_____

_____

_____

_____

_____

Lists for Our Family

Books to read together...

_____

_____

_____

_____

_____

_____

_____

_____

_____

_____

LISTS TO LIVE BY

Lists for Our Family

Ways to show we love each other...

_____

_____

_____

_____

_____

_____

_____

_____

_____

Lists for Our Family

Projects to do together...

_____

_____

_____

_____

_____

_____

_____

_____

_____

_____

Lists for Our Family

Places to visit together...

_____

_____

_____

_____

_____

_____

_____

_____

_____

_____

Lists for Our Family

Gifts to give one another...

_____

_____

_____

_____

_____

_____

_____

_____

_____

Life-changing advice
in a quick-to-read format!

LISTS TO LIVE BY

Lists to Live By, Vol. 1

This treasury of to-the-point inspiration—two hundred lists—is loaded with invaluable insights for success, friendships, family, contentment, wisdom, and more. These wide-ranging ideas can change your life!

ISBN 1-57673-478-1

Lists to Live By, Vol. 2

You'll get a lift in a hurry as you browse through this treasure-trove of more *Lists to Live By*—with wisdom for home, health, love, life, faith, and successful living.

ISBN 1-57673-685-7

LISTS TO LIVE BY FOR EVERY MARRIED COUPLE

compiled by Alice Gray, Steve Stephens, and John Van Diest

Love and Logic for the Happy Couple

On-the-go wives and husbands who seek a burst of inspiration or encouragement for their relationship will find just what they need in *Lists to Live By for Every Married Couple*. Eighty lists, compiled by three respected authors, provide couples with insights on love, communication, romance, fun, forgiveness, making memories, and more. More than another trivia book, *Lists* offers tender, romantic, and wise ways to bring new life to marriage in a popular, easy-to-read format. This latest collection of *Lists to Live By* is filled with gems of inspiration and timeless truths that married couples will treasure and use for a lifetime.

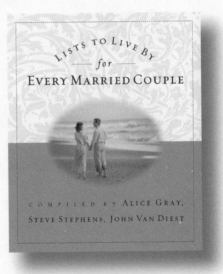

ISBN 1-57673-998-8

Acknowledgments

Hundreds of books and magazines were researched, and dozens of professionals were interviewed for this collection. A diligent effort has been made to attribute original ownership of each list and, when necessary, obtain permission to reprint. If we have overlooked giving proper credit to anyone, please accept our apologies. If you will contact Multnomah Publishers, Inc., Post Office Box 1720, Sisters, Oregon 97759, with written documentation, corrections will be made prior to additional printings.

Notes and acknowledgments in this bibliography are shown in the order the lists appear, and in the styles designated by the sources. For permission to reprint material, please request permission from the original source. The editors gratefully acknowledge authors, publishers, and agents who granted permission for reprinting these lists.

Lists without attribution were compiled by the editors.